D1564119

CONNECT

THE ELECTION OF 1860: A NATION DIVIDES ON THE EVE OF WAR

by Jessica Gunderson

Consultant:
Dennis Showalter, PhD
Professor of History
Colorado College

CAPSTONE PRESS
a capstone imprint

Connect is published by Capstone Press,
1710 Roe Crest Drive, North Mankato, Minnesota 56003
www.capstonepub.com

Library of Congress Cataloging-in-Publication Data
Gunderson, Jessica, author.
  The Election of 1860: A Nation Divides on the Eve of War/by Jessica Gunderson.
       pages cm.—(Connect. Presidential Politics)
  Summary: "With the election of 1860, the issue of slavery finally came to a head,
setting the stage for the American Civil War. Compelling, action-packed text, vivid
sensory details, and primary source quotes bring the story to life so that readers feel
as if they were actually alive during the historical event"—Provided by publisher.
  Includes bibliographical references and index.
  Audience: Age 8–14.
  Audience: Grades 4 to 6.
  ISBN 978-1-4914-8240-7 (library binding)
  ISBN 978-1-4914-8630-6 (paperback)
  ISBN 978-1-4914-8651-1 (ebook PDF)
  1. Presidents—United States—Election—1860—Juvenile literature. United States—
Politics and government—1857–1861—Juvenile literature. Lincoln, Abraham, 1809–
1865—Political career before 1861—Juvenile literature.
  LCC E440 .G86 2016
  324.97309/034—dc23   2015038464

Editorial Credits
Jennifer Huston, editor; Veronica Scott, designer; Tracy Cummins, media researcher;
Kathy McColley, production specialist

Photo Credits
Alamy: Bygone Collection, 32, Classic Image, 11, Old Paper Studios, 6, 20–21, World
History Archive, 36; Capstone Press: 34; Corbis: 4–5, 33, 44; Detroit Public Library/
Burton Historical Collection: 31; Getty Images: Bob Thomas/Popperfoto, 37, Hulton
Archive, 43 Left; Library of Congress: Cover Left, Cover Middle Left, Cover Middle
Right, 13, 16, 18, 22, 23 Bottom Right, 23 Top Left, 23 Top Right, 24, 25, 26, 27, 28, 29,
30 Top, 38–39, 40, 42, 45; Newscom: Album/sfgp, 7, Mathew Brady/Picture History,
14, Picture History, 35, UIG Universal Images Group, 23 Bottom Left; Shutterstock:
catwalker, 43 Right, Everett Historical, 9, 19, 41, javarman, Design Element,
Marzolino, 30 Bottom, watcharakun, Design Element; Wikimedia: Alexander Hessler,
12, Library of Congress Prints and Photographs Division/AJCham, Cover Right, 8,
NARA, 15, Tintazul: Júlio Reis, 10

Printed in the United States of America in North Mankato, Minnesota.
009221CGS16

TABLE OF CONTENTS

CHAPTER 1

THE BOILING POINT

On a cold February night in 1860, a tall, thin man took the stage at the Cooper Union building's Great Hall in New York City. The crowd fell silent as he spoke.

"Can we … allow [slavery] to spread?" the man asked. His voice was strong and calm. "If our sense of duty forbids this, then let us stand by our duty, fearlessly and effectively." According to the Constitution, he explained, the government must prevent the spread of slavery. When he finished speaking, the audience broke into thunderous applause. They tossed their hats into the air and waved handkerchiefs. The man's straightforward and clear words impressed and excited them. Who was this man? Few had heard his name before.

Several presidents, including Theodore Roosevelt, Bill Clinton, and Barack Obama, have given speeches in the Great Hall of the Cooper Union building in New York City.

The man was Abraham Lincoln, a former U.S. representative from Illinois. He had recently entered the political stage as a presidential hopeful. Two years earlier, in 1858, he had challenged U.S. Senator Stephen Douglas for his Senate seat. The two went face-to-face in a series of **debates** all across Illinois. Douglas was a popular and persuasive speaker, and many were stunned at Lincoln's skill at debating him. In the end Lincoln lost the Senate race. But he continued to speak about political matters and slavery.

Abe Lincoln speaks during one of the Lincoln–Douglas debates. Stephen Douglas stands behind him.

The Slavery Question

For decades, the issue of slavery had the nation tangled in bitter conflict. Slavery was part of the southern way of life. Southern plantation owners relied upon unpaid slaves to plant and harvest crops. Although slavery was illegal in many northern states, the northern economy benefited from slavery as well. Northern factories and **textile** mills turned raw cotton from the South into finished goods. Because slaves weren't paid, slave labor helped keep the price of cotton low, which allowed northern industries to profit.

By 1850, nearly 75 percent of slaves forced to work in the agriculture industry in the United States labored on cotton plantations.

debate—a polite discussion on something people disagree about
textile—a fabric or cloth that has been woven or knitted

In the 1830s the **abolitionist** movement began sweeping across the North. Abolitionists believed slavery was morally wrong and should be illegal. They gave moving speeches and published antislavery pamphlets. *Uncle Tom's Cabin*, a book by Harriet Beecher Stowe that told of the horrors of slavery, quickly became a best seller.

Politically, the hottest topic was the expansion of slavery. The young nation was growing at a rapid pace, and thousands of settlers were moving westward. The question on everyone's mind was whether or not slavery should be allowed in new states and **territories**.

Uncle Tom's Cabin opened the eyes of Northerners to the cruelty of slavery. The book was banned in the South.

UNCLE TOM'S CABIN;

OR,

LIFE AMONG THE LOWLY.

BY

HARRIET BEECHER STOWE.

VOL. I.

ONE HUNDRED AND FIFTH THOUSAND.

BOSTON:
JOHN P. JEWETT & COMPANY
CLEVELAND, OHIO:
JEWETT, PROCTOR & WORTHINGTON.
1852.

abolitionist—a person who worked to end slavery
territory—an area belonging to the United States that is not a state

As a whole, the nation was split on the answer to that question. Some believed that the settlers of the state or territory should vote on the issue. Others believed the federal government should decide.

Expanding slavery to new states wasn't just a moral issue. Northerners worried that the South would have too much political power if there were more slave states. Southerners had similar concerns about northern power. Maintaining an equal number of free and slave states was important to keeping peace.

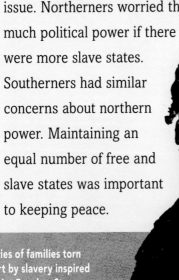

Stories of families torn apart by slavery inspired Harriet Beecher Stowe to write her famous novel, *Uncle Tom's Cabin*.

Congress passed various acts to encourage such agreement. The Missouri Compromise of 1820 added Missouri as a slave state and Maine as a free state. It also banned slavery in any new state above the 36°30' parallel. The compromise helped keep a balance between the number of slave and free states.

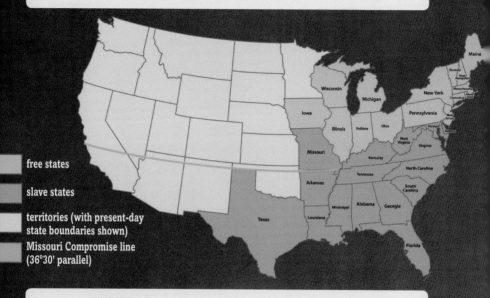

free states

slave states

territories (with present-day state boundaries shown)

Missouri Compromise line (36°30' parallel)

In 1854 the Kansas–Nebraska Act passed. It allowed the settlers of Kansas and Nebraska to decide whether or not to permit slavery. It also went against the Missouri Compromise because both territories were above the 36°30' parallel.

As a result, pro-slavery and antislavery settlers flocked to Kansas. Both groups wanted to outvote the other on the issue of slavery. Anger led to physical violence. Settlers killed each other and set fire to buildings and homesteads.

The bloody clashes in Kansas horrified the nation. Americans were now killing each other over slavery. The issue could no longer be ignored.

Things turned violent in Kansas as settlers disagreed over the issue of slavery.

Fugitive Slave Act of 1850

By the mid-1800s, thousands of slaves had run away from their masters and escaped to the North to freedom. The Fugitive Slave Act of 1793 required that any runaway slaves be returned to their owners. However, many northern states passed laws to get around this act.

The Fugitive Slave Act of 1850 strengthened the old law. It said that anyone who helped a runaway slave would be punished—even if the slave had reached a free state. In addition, those who captured and returned runaway slaves received a reward. A flood of slave hunters invaded the North to track down and capture anyone suspected of being a former slave.

At the time, even free blacks had no legal right to defend themselves in court and prove they were free. As a result, many free African-Americans were forced into slavery. The act angered many Northerners who didn't want to enforce slavery.

CHAPTER 2

CONVENTIONS AND SURPRISES

Democrat James Buchanan of Pennsylvania, a northern state, was elected president in 1856. Because he did not take a firm stand on the issue of slavery, he was viewed as a weak president. As a result, he did not seek re-election. Instead, new candidates competed for the office, and Americans held their breath. They knew the next president would face many challenges. But they had no idea that the country was about to fall apart.

In the spring of 1860, the presidential campaign was underway. Workers in Chicago hammered day and night, quickly building a large meeting hall known as "the Wigwam." In just a few short weeks, thousands of Republicans would pour into Chicago for the party's national **convention**.

The Wigwam, the site of the 1860 Republican convention, burned down in 1869.

South Carolina formally seceded from the Union at Institute Hall in Charleston. In December 1861, the building burned in a fire that destroyed much of the city.

Meanwhile, in Charleston, South Carolina, Democrats filled Institute Hall to the brim. At the end of April, the Democratic convention was in full swing. But northern and southern party members did not agree on many issues, particularly slavery. The Southerners spoke out against Stephen Douglas, the Northerners' choice for president. Douglas had helped pass the Compromise of 1850 and the Kansas–Nebraska Act, which tried to please both sides with a compromise.

convention—a large gathering of people who have the same interests
secede—to formally withdraw from a group or an organization

But the Southern Democrats did not want compromise. They were very much in favor of slavery. They wanted the Democratic **platform** to include a federal slave code—a law protecting slavery in all U.S. territories. They believed that slaveholders should be able to move their slaves into the new territories if they wished.

Northern Democrats knew that northern voters would not accept a pro-slavery platform. They rejected the idea of a federal slave code.

Enraged, 50 southern **delegates** stormed out of the convention hall. Their dramatic exit left the Democratic convention in an uproar. Without the Southerners, the Northern Democrats didn't have enough delegates to **nominate** Stephen Douglas. The convention ended, and the Democrats planned to meet again in June in Baltimore.

Stephen Douglas

platform—a statement of political goals made by members of a political party
delegate—a person who represents a larger group of people at a meeting
nominate—to suggest that someone would be the right person to do a job

REPUBLICAN CONTENDERS

Shortly after the dramatic dividing of the Democratic Party, the Republican convention began on May 16. Because the Democrats were split, the Republican candidate had a good chance of winning the presidency.

All eyes turned to the Republican front-runner, William H. Seward, a powerful political figure. He'd been a U.S. senator and served as governor of New York. However, in recent years, he'd made **radical** statements to drive home his antislavery beliefs. Southerners viewed some of his statements as a threat of war.

William H. Seward

radical—extreme compared to what most people think or do

Despite Seward's extreme views, his supporters were confident that he'd win the nomination. Of the leading contenders, which included Simon Cameron, Edward Bates, Salmon P. Chase, and Abraham Lincoln, Seward had the most political experience. But Seward and his supporters underestimated the lanky lawyer from Illinois.

Simon Cameron

Edward Bates

Salmon P. Chase

LITTLE-KNOWN LINCOLN

Abraham Lincoln had little experience in national politics. He'd served only a brief time in the U.S. House of Representatives (1847–1849). Then he'd lost the Senate race to Stephen Douglas in 1858. But he'd gained national fame for his speeches, especially those that demonstrated his views on slavery.

Some Republicans wanted an immediate end to slavery. But Lincoln's views were more **moderate**. He believed slavery was wrong, and he opposed the spread of slavery. But he also believed the U.S. Constitution protected slavery where it was already in place. Lincoln's plan was to remain moderate and avoid attacking his fellow Republicans' views.

Lincoln's **strategy** proved successful. Seward, Cameron, Chase, and Bates had all annoyed various members of the party with their extreme views. But Lincoln's more moderate views appealed to many.

moderate—avoiding extremes of behavior or expression
strategy—a careful plan or method

The location of the Republican convention also gave Lincoln a slight advantage. He had sweeping support in his home state of Illinois. In fact, before the convention, his campaigners printed extra tickets and handed them out for free. When the event began, the Wigwam was packed with Lincoln supporters.

Lincoln was at home in Springfield, Illinois, during the convention. At the time, candidates didn't attend the conventions, even if they expected to win. At home, Lincoln patiently awaited the results of the convention.

"I am not the first choice of a very great many."
—Abraham Lincoln

When the delegates began to vote, Lincoln fans let out a

deafening roar. Because of the extra tickets Lincoln's supporters had handed out, his fans outnumbered Seward's. Even so, those backing Seward thought their candidate had the nomination in the bag. But they were wrong.

Lincoln's home in Springfield, Illinois

In the first round of voting, Seward received 173 votes. Lincoln received 102 votes. Cameron had 50, Chase had 49, Bates had 48, and the rest fell to minor candidates. But in order to win, the nominee needed 234 votes—one more than half the total number of votes. Seward didn't have it, so the delegates voted again. This time, Seward and Lincoln were neck and neck. Seward had 184 votes, and Lincoln had 181.

Before becoming president, Abe Lincoln did not have a beard.

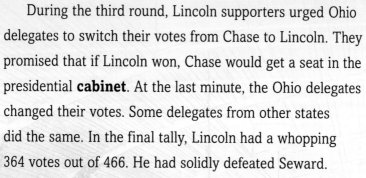

During the third round, Lincoln supporters urged Ohio delegates to switch their votes from Chase to Lincoln. They promised that if Lincoln won, Chase would get a seat in the presidential **cabinet**. At the last minute, the Ohio delegates changed their votes. Some delegates from other states did the same. In the final tally, Lincoln had a whopping 364 votes out of 466. He had solidly defeated Seward.

After a moment of stunned silence, Lincoln fans stomped their feet and cheered. Church bells rang throughout Chicago. A cannon fired from atop the Wigwam. The Republican Party had a candidate!

cabinet—a group of officials who give advice to the president
inaugurate—to swear an official into public office

When Lincoln heard the news, he said, with his typical humor, "There is a little woman at our house who is probably more interested in this [news] than I am." That night, a cheering crowd surrounded his home. When he told the crowd his house was too small to let them all inside, someone shouted, "We will give you a larger house [the White House] on the fourth of next March!" That's when presidents were **inaugurated** until the 20th Amendment to the Constitution was adopted in 1933.

A PARTY DIVIDED

Meanwhile, the Democrats still hadn't chosen a presidential candidate. When the Democratic Party met in Baltimore in June, tempers flared once again. A fight broke out over whom to nominate and whether to propose a federal slave code. Again, many southern delegates left the meeting. The remaining delegates nominated Stephen Douglas. Southern Democrats then held their own meeting and chose John C. Breckinridge as their candidate.

Another candidate also emerged at this time. The Constitutional Union Party believed in upholding the Constitution and preserving the Union, or keeping the states united as one country. They took no stand on the issue of slavery, hoping that ignoring it would gain them votes. They nominated John Bell of Tennessee for president.

Now four candidates were battling for the presidency. Each man faced a tough contest, and the winner would hold the fate of the United States in his hands.

Stephen Douglas

John Bell

John C. Breckinridge

Abraham Lincoln

CHAPTER 3

MEET THE CANDIDATES

At age 63, John Bell was the oldest of the four presidential candidates. He'd been involved in politics most of his adult life. He'd served as a U.S. representative, a senator, and secretary of war.

Although he was a slave owner, Bell was against expanding slavery to new states and territories. He believed in the Constitutional Union Party's slogan, "The Union as it is, and the Constitution as it is."

A campaign poster for the Constitutional Union Party shows John Bell and vice presidential candidate Edward Everett with their hands placed on the U.S. Constitution.

Bell had some support in the northern states, so Southerners called him a "friend of abolitionists." Bell knew he was the underdog, so he didn't campaign much. He hoped that none of the candidates would gain enough votes to win. If that happened, then, according to the Constitution, the House of Representatives would determine the winner. That was the only way Bell might stand a chance.

VICE PRESIDENT FOR PRESIDENT

John C. Breckinridge was the South's leading contender. Born and raised in Kentucky, he came from a long line of politicians. Breckinridge served in the Mexican War (1846–1848) and then became a U.S. representative. He was also the current vice president of the United States under James Buchanan.

DEMOCRATIC TICKET

OUR PRINCIPLES
The Constitution

The Sovereignty & Equality of the States; The Repeal of the Missouri Restriction; The People of the Territories in forming State Governments to adopt their own Institutions. Equal protection to Citizens Native & Naturalized, & to every species of Property.

FOR PRESIDENT
JOHN C. BRECKINRIDGE
of Kentucky
FOR VICE PRESIDENT
JOSEPH LANE
of Oregon
ELECTORS

Southern Democratic candidate John C. Breckinridge was the cousin of Abraham Lincoln's wife.

Breckinridge and Buchanan didn't get along. The president rarely invited Breckinridge to meetings or asked his advice on political matters. However, their dislike for one another actually worked in Breckinridge's favor. The nation had grown to despise Buchanan, so when his popularity dropped, Breckinridge's rose.

"THE LITTLE GIANT"

Stephen Douglas, the Northern Democratic candidate, was Lincoln's main opponent in the North. Because of his short stature and loud, booming voice, he'd been nicknamed "the Little Giant." Douglas had served in both the U.S. House of Representatives and the U.S. Senate. He was a strong believer in compromise between the North and South. He helped get the Compromise of 1850 and the Kansas–Nebraska Act passed. By 1860, he was the best-known senator in the nation.

Stephen Douglas, the Little Giant

The Compromise of 1850

The Compromise of 1850 was a group of bills passed by Congress to help keep peace between free and slave states. The Compromise admitted California to the Union as a free state. It also allowed the new territories of Utah and New Mexico to decide whether or not to allow slavery within their borders. The Compromise also contained the controversial Fugitive Slave Act of 1850.

HONEST ABE

Abraham Lincoln was quite different from the other candidates. He didn't come from a long line of politicians. In fact, he came from rather humble beginnings.

Abraham Lincoln was born on February 12, 1809, in a one-room log cabin in rural Kentucky. A few years later, his family moved to Indiana. Abe's mother died when he was 9. A few months later, his father married a widow with three children of her own.

Abe Lincoln's birthplace

Abraham and his father, Thomas, had a troubled relationship. Abe loved books and enjoyed learning. Thomas didn't understand his son's love of books, and the two often quarreled. Abraham grew close to his stepmother, Sally, who encouraged his reading.

Abe's father, Thomas Lincoln

A Lucky Save

Abraham Lincoln was named after his grandfather Abraham, a Revolutionary War captain. After the war, Captain Lincoln moved his young family to Kentucky. While he was tending the fields with his three sons, an American Indian fired a gun from the woods nearby. Captain Lincoln fell to the ground dead. His oldest son, Mordecai, ran to get a gun. When he returned, he saw an Indian emerge from the woods and reach for the youngest boy, Thomas. Mordecai shot and killed the man, saving his brother from capture. Young Thomas grew up to become the father of Abraham Lincoln.

Abraham Lincoln's upbringing in the wilderness generated legends and stories. In one popular story, as a shopkeeper Lincoln walked miles to return money to a customer who had overpaid. Tales of his honesty earned him the nickname "Honest Abe."

When Thomas moved his family to Illinois in 1830, 21-year-old Abraham went too. But once there, he struck out on his own to make a living.

Abraham had grown into a tall, strong young man. His first job was splitting wood for firewood and fences. Later he worked as a postmaster, shopkeeper, and store owner.

Abraham loved to tell stories and jokes to his customers. His popularity led him to seek a career in law and to get involved in state politics.

In the 1858 Senate race, Honest Abe squared off against the Little Giant, Stephen Douglas. Two years later, the men faced each other again in one of the most important presidential elections in history.

CHAPTER 4

CAMPAIGNING FOR THE VOTE

In the 1800s, candidates didn't campaign for themselves as they do today. They were expected to stay out of sight while others campaigned for them.

During the 1860 campaign, Lincoln rarely left his home in Springfield. Instead, he conducted a "front porch" campaign. He sat on his porch and talked to anyone who came to visit him. When they asked about his political views, he often told them to read his published speeches.

Lincoln's supporters campaigned with enthusiasm. In October 1860, thousands of young men known as "Wide Awakes" marched through Chicago in support of Lincoln. Campaigners also held parades, rallies, and picnics. They encouraged citizens to vote for "Honest Abe." Some even carried wooden poles or rails to remind voters of Lincoln's hardworking past as a wood splitter.

A group known as the Wide Awakes were among the many Lincoln supporters.

Lincoln's opponents often made fun of his rustic upbringing. They said he was only good for chopping wood, not for being president. They also made fun of his looks, calling him "**homely.**"

"Let Your Whiskers Grow"

In October 1860, 11-year-old Grace Bedell wrote Abraham Lincoln a letter telling him he should grow a beard to fill out his thin face. Ladies liked whiskers, Grace wrote, and they would tell their husbands to vote for him. When he received the letter, Lincoln responded right away, saying he was unsure about growing whiskers. He'd never had a beard before. But right after the election, he took Grace's advice and let his beard grow.

On his way to Washington in 1861, Lincoln stopped in Grace's hometown in New York. A crowd gathered to see the new president. Lincoln told the story of Grace's letter and asked if she was in the crowd. When Grace came forward, he kissed her on the cheek as the audience cheered with delight.

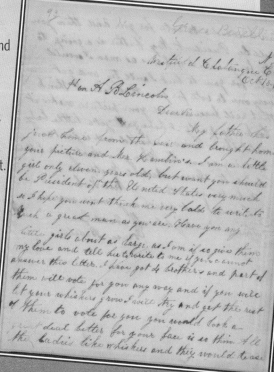

homely—plain, or unattractive

Abolitionists were not pleased with Lincoln either. They wanted a president who would ban slavery altogether, not just prevent it from spreading.

ON THE TRAIL

Unlike his opponents, Stephen Douglas hit the campaign trail himself. He announced that he was going to visit his mother in New York. On the way, he stopped at several cities to give speeches. Opponents made fun of Douglas' "search for his mother," but he continued on. He traveled the country, sometimes giving two or three speeches a day. When he campaigned in the Deep South, opponents threw rotten fruit and eggs at him.

Fearing a Republican win, Southern Democrats proposed a plan. Douglas, Breckinridge, and Bell would withdraw, and a single candidate would take their place. Breckinridge and Bell agreed, but Douglas would not back down, so the plan was called off.

Northern Democrat Stephen Douglas and his running mate Herschel V. Johnson

THE NATION DECIDES

On Tuesday, November 6, 1860, voters headed to the polls. About 81 percent of **eligible** voters cast their ballots. It was the highest voter turnout in history at the time. In fact, it is still the second-highest voter turnout in U.S. history. The election of 1876 drew less than 1 percent more voters than the election of 1860.

eligible—qualified to participate

Crowds in New York City wait outside a newspaper office to hear the results of the election of 1860.

In the North many voted for Lincoln, hoping that he would hold the nation together and solve the slavery problem. They admired his plain and honest views. However, in most southern states, Lincoln's name wasn't even on the ballot. Voters in the Deep South voted for Breckinridge. In the Upper South, or border states, votes were split among Bell, Breckinridge, and Douglas.

Candidate	Popular Votes	Electoral Votes
Abraham Lincoln (Republican)	1,865,908	180
John C. Breckinridge (Southern Democrat)	848,019	72
John Bell (Constitutional Union Party)	590,901	39
Stephen Douglas (Northern Democrat)	1,380,202	12

Abraham Lincoln did not plan to vote. He felt it was improper to vote for himself. But his law partner reminded him that state officials were also on the ballot. After some thought, Lincoln headed to the polls.

THE CHOSEN LEADER

After the **popular votes** were counted, delegates from the **Electoral College** cast votes for each state. Lincoln won the election easily. He earned 180 out of 303 electoral votes, although he only needed 153 to win. He also received nearly 40 percent of the popular vote. The United States had a new leader—Abraham Lincoln, the very first Republican president.

Even if the Democratic Party hadn't split, Lincoln still would have won the election. With a single candidate on the ballot, the Democratic Party would have won the popular vote. But because of the states that Lincoln won in the North, the Democrats still would've lost the electoral vote, which is what decides presidential elections. The election of 1860 showed how important the heavily populated northern states are to winning the presidency.

The next day, after hearing of his victory, Lincoln went to the governor's office in Springfield to greet visitors. Sitting in a chair with his feet propped against a large stove, he spoke to everyone who stopped by. When a group of young men came by to congratulate him, he said, "Well, boys, your troubles are over, but mine have just begun."

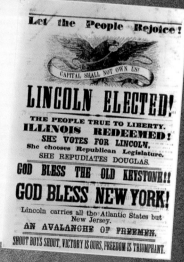

popular vote—the number of voters who vote for a candidate in a general election
Electoral College—the group of people that elects the president and vice president after the general election

CHAPTER 5

VICTORY AND DEATH

Lincoln was right. His troubles were just beginning. After the election, Southerners were filled with anger. "The South alone should govern the South!" became their battle cry. They believed southern interests were threatened with Lincoln as president.

On December 20, 1860, just six weeks after Lincoln's election, South Carolina seceded from the Union. Other states soon followed suit.

Southerners protested and rallied to secede from the Union when Lincoln became president.

OFF TO WASHINGTON

In February 1861, Lincoln left his home in Springfield and boarded a train for Washington, D.C. His wife, Mary, and their three sons accompanied him. Thousands of people turned out to catch a glimpse of the new president as he made his way to the nation's capital.

On March 4, 1861, on the steps of the U.S. Capitol, Lincoln was sworn in as the nation's 16th president. A huge crowd gathered to watch the event.

"If you are as happy in entering the White House as I shall feel [leaving it], you are a happy man."
—James Buchanan to Abraham Lincoln

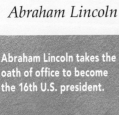

Abraham Lincoln takes the oath of office to become the 16th U.S. president.

After taking the oath of office, Lincoln began his **inaugural address**. He had spent weeks preparing his speech and chose his words carefully. He hoped the South was listening. His main goal was to preserve the Union and prevent war. But by that time, seven states had already left the Union and formed the Confederate States of America.

In his speech, Lincoln stated that he had no plans to interfere with slavery in the southern states. He also said he would not fire upon the South unless the South fired first. And he reminded his listeners that, according to the Constitution, seceding was illegal. As his speech drew to a close, he said, "We are not enemies, but friends. We must not be enemies."

Unfortunately, the South ignored Lincoln's pleas. In April the Confederate army fired on U.S. troops stationed at Fort Sumter in South Carolina. Lincoln sent 75,000 **reinforcements**. The South viewed this act as a declaration of war, and four more states seceded. The Civil War had begun.

inaugural address—the speech a president gives when he or she is sworn into office
reinforcements—extra troops sent into battle

THE FATE OF THE CONTENDERS

John C. Breckinridge had lost the presidential race but had been elected to the Senate. He urged Lincoln to withdraw U.S. troops from the South. He thought the United States should allow the southern states to secede peacefully rather than wage war against them. Breckinridge eventually left his Senate seat and became a Confederate general. The United States officially declared him a traitor.

John C. Breckinridge

Stephen Douglas agreed that Lincoln should aim to preserve the Union. He gave patriotic speeches in support of Lincoln and the Union. However, Douglas died only a few months after the Civil War began.

John Bell initially believed the Union should be preserved. But when Lincoln sent Union troops to the South after the battle of Fort Sumter, Bell was furious. He decided to support the Confederacy and urged his home state of Tennessee to secede.

Lincoln and his cabinet (from left to right): Edwin Stanton, Salmon P. Chase, Lincoln, Gideon Wells, Caleb Smith, William H. Seward, Montgomery Blair, Edward Bates

FACT

As president, Lincoln gave each of his Republican opponents a job in his cabinet. Seward was named secretary of state, Cameron became secretary of war, Chase was secretary of the treasury, and Bates was his attorney general.

THE WAR BETWEEN THE STATES

The Civil War lasted longer than anyone expected it would. For four long years, brutal battles took place between the North and the South. In some cases, families were torn apart as brothers fought against brothers and fathers fought against sons. More than 600,000 soldiers died in the war, and nearly as many were injured but survived.

Lincoln was troubled by so much death, but he stuck to his goal of preserving the Union. In 1863 he issued the Emancipation Proclamation, which freed slaves in the seceded states. Lincoln regarded the Emancipation Proclamation as his greatest accomplishment.

Emancipation Proclamation

Lincoln's Emancipation Proclamation declared that all slaves in states that had seceded were forever free. Slaves across the South rejoiced. With the help of Union soldiers, many slaves left their masters. Some joined the Union army and helped win the war. The proclamation boosted support for the war among Northerners. Now the war was not only about preserving the Union but also about freeing slaves.

But not all slaves became free with the Emancipation Proclamation. The proclamation did not apply to slaves in border states that had not seceded from the Union. The proclamation was only the first step in freeing slaves. First, the North had to win the war. In 1865, after the war, Congress passed the 13th Amendment. The amendment legally banned slavery in all states and territories.

Lincoln's Emancipation Proclamation promised freedom for all Americans.

THE BEGINNING OF THE END

Lincoln was re-elected in 1864, winning more than 55 percent of the popular vote. In his second inaugural speech, Lincoln promised to rebuild the nation.

On April 9, 1865, one month after Lincoln's second term began, Confederate General Robert E. Lee surrendered to U.S. General Ulysses S. Grant. The Civil War was over.

Five days later, Lincoln attended a play with his wife. He was exhausted from the burdens of war, but he was also hopeful for the future. One of his hopes was to repair relations with the South. When he took his seat in the presidential box at Ford's Theatre, the audience gave him a standing ovation. But it was the last applause Lincoln would ever receive. That night, Confederate sympathizer John Wilkes Booth crept into the presidential box and shot Lincoln in the head. The president died the following morning, on April 15, 1865.

John Wilkes Booth assassinates Abraham Lincoln.

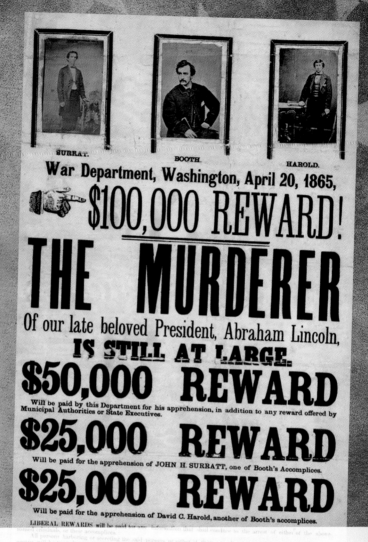

SURRAT.   BOOTH.   HAROLD.

War Department, Washington, April 20, 1865,

$100,000 REWARD!

THE MURDERER

Of our late beloved President, Abraham Lincoln,

IS STILL AT LARGE.

$50,000 REWARD

Will be paid by this Department for his apprehension, in addition to any reward offered by
Municipal Authorities or State Executives.

$25,000 REWARD

Will be paid for the apprehension of JOHN H. SURRATT, one of Booth's Accomplices.

$25,000 REWARD

Will be paid for the apprehension of David C. Harold, another of Booth's accomplices.

LIBERAL REWARDS will be paid for any information that shall conduce to the arrest of either of the above-

Abraham Lincoln started from humble beginnings to become the most powerful man in the United States. In a few short years, he rose from an unknown politician to the most famous man in the country. Although his election sparked a tragic war, he never gave up on his goal of preserving the Union. In the midst of war, he issued freedom to all slaves with a northern victory. "Honest Abe" had become the "Great Emancipator."

GLOSSARY

abolitionist (ab-uh-LISH-uh-nist)—a person who worked to end slavery

cabinet (KAB-uh-nit)—a group of officials who give advice to the president

convention (kuhn-VEN-shuhn)—a large gathering of people who have the same interests

debate (di-BATE)—a polite discussion on something people disagree about

delegate (DEL-i-git)—a person who represents a larger group of people at a meeting

Electoral College (ee-lehk-TOHR-uhl KAH-lij)—the group of people that elects the president and vice president after the general election

eligible (EL-i-juh-buhl)—qualified to participate

homely (HOME-lee)—plain, or unattractive

inaugural address (in-AW-gyuh-ruhl ad-DRESS)—the speech a president gives when he or she is sworn into office

inaugurate (in-AW-gyuh-rate)—to swear an official into public office

moderate (MAH-dur-it)—avoiding extremes of behavior or expression

nominate (NAH-muh-nate)—to suggest that someone would be the right person to do a job

platform (PLAT-form)—a statement of political goals made by members of a political party

popular vote (PAHP-yuh-lur VOHT)—the number of voters who vote for a candidate in a general election

radical (RAD-i-kuhl)—extreme compared to what most people think or do

reinforcements (ree-in-FORS-muhnts)—extra troops sent into battle

secede (si-SEED)—to formally withdraw from a group or an organization, often to form another organization

strategy (STRAT-i-jee)—a careful plan or method

territory (TER-i-tor-ee)—an area belonging to the United States that is not a state

textile (TEK-stile)—a fabric or cloth that has been woven or knitted

READ MORE

Hall, Brianna. *Freedom from Slavery: Causes and Effects of the Emancipation Proclamation*. North Mankato, Minn.: Capstone Press, 2014.

Schroeder, Alan. *Abe Lincoln: His Wit and Wisdom from A–Z*. New York: Holiday House, 2015.

Sobel, Syl. *Presidential Elections and Other Cool Facts*. Hauppauge, N.Y.: Barron's Educational Series, 2012.

CRITICAL THINKING USING THE COMMON CORE

1. Describe why Lincoln's election prompted southern states to leave the Union. Use details from the book to support your ideas. (Key Ideas and Details)

2. Describe what the word "compromise" means. Why weren't the North and South able to compromise? (Craft and Structure)

3. Compare and contrast the beliefs of two presidential candidates of 1860: Abraham Lincoln, Stephen Douglas, John C. Breckinridge, or John Bell. (Integration of Knowledge and Ideas)

INDEX

INTERNET SITES

FactHound offers a safe, fun way to find Internet sites related to this book. All of the sites on FactHound have been researched by our staff.

Here's all you do:
Visit *www.facthound.com*
Type in this code: 9781491482407